Epictetus's Raven

Alice Brière-Haquet

Plexicut illustrations by Csil

OH EDITIONS

INTRODUCTION

Epictetus (c. 50–c. 135 AD) was a Greek Stoic philosopher. He believed philosophy was not just a theoretical study but a way of life too. To Epictetus, things that lie beyond our control should be of no particular concern and so should cause neither anger nor grief. We are responsible for our own actions and attitudes, though, so we should be concerned about how to live. In fact, the only thing we truly own and that is of ethical significance to ourselves is our own conduct. Epictetus didn't write down his own teachings, but instead they were recorded by his student, Arrian of Nicomedia.

In this story, Epictetus is reminding us to focus only on what we can control – our own conduct – and not spend time worrying about what we can't control. Happiness can only be achieved when we accept what we can't control and endeavor to conduct ourselves as ethically as we should.

Somewhere on a rooftop,
a raven caws.

The greatest scholars
gather and comment
on the event.

Was the cry coming from
the left or from the right?
Is this a good or a bad omen?

They draw a map of the stars,
they interpret the
poems of old prophets,
to better understand what
the gods meant.

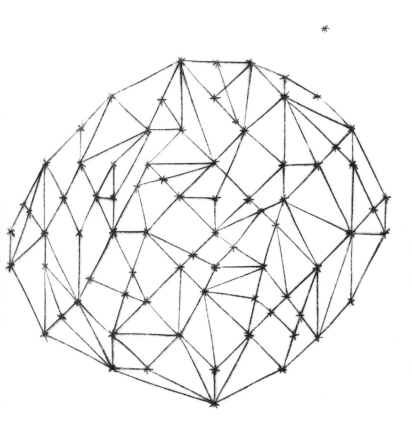

Are they announcing a battle?
A tornado? A storm?
Perhaps the end of an era?
Should we sound the alarm?

A new caw. The discussion becomes urgent.

Then a wise man steps forward.

"These omens are not for me:
they concern my fields, my house,
my money.

If all this prospers, I will be richer.

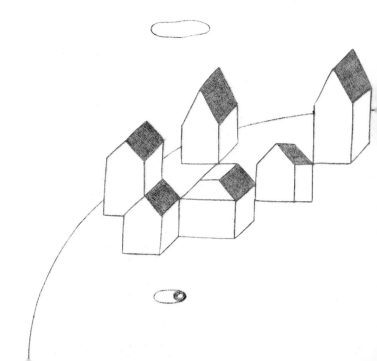

If all this is lost, I will be freer.

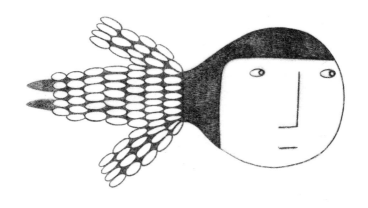
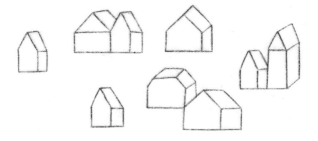

So whatever happens, my happiness does not depend on it.

What does the message of
the gods matter to us?
Let's look for what is beautiful
in the crow's song...

...and try to be happy."

OTHER TITLES IN THE
POCKET PHILOSOPHY SERIES:

Heidegger's Lizard
by Alice Brière-Haquet and
illustrated by Sophie Vissière

Schopenhauer's Porcupine
by Alice Brière-Haquet and illustrated
by Olivier Philipponneau

Zhuangzi's Butterfly
by Alice Brière-Haquet and
illustrated by Raphaële Enjary